# Mary McLeod Bethune
## VOICE OF BLACK HOPE

"I had faith in a living God, faith in myself, and a desire to serve."          —Mary McLeod Bethune

*Praise for the* Women of Our Time® *Series*

"Highly regarded authors ... appear in the roster of contributors to 'Women of Our Time.'"          —*Parents Magazine*

"Packs plenty of interest and facts into a brief format for young readers."          —*Christian Science Monitor*

"Provides insight into diverse personalities ... Accessible, attractive, and balanced ... A welcome resource."          —*The Horn Book*

# Mary McLeod Bethune

VOICE OF BLACK HOPE

BY MILTON MELTZER

ILLUSTRATED BY STEPHEN MARCHESI

PUFFIN BOOKS

*In memory of George Hill*     M.M.

PUFFIN BOOKS

Published by the Penguin Group

Penguin Putnam Inc., 375 Hudson Street, New York, New York 10014, U.S.A.

Penguin Books Ltd, 27 Wrights Lane, London W8 5TZ, England

Penguin Books Australia Ltd, Ringwood, Victoria, Australia

Penguin Books Canada Ltd, 10 Alcorn Avenue, Toronto, Ontario, Canada M4V 3B2

Penguin Books (N.Z.) Ltd, 182–190 Wairau Road, Auckland 10, New Zealand

Penguin Books Ltd, Registered Offices: Harmondsworth, Middlesex, England

First published by Viking Penguin Inc., 1987
Published in Puffin Books 1988

30  29  28  27  26  25

Text copyright © Milton Meltzer, 1987
Illustrations copyright © Stephen Marchesi, 1987
All rights reserved

*Women of Our Time*® is a registered trademark of Viking Penguin Inc.
Printed in the United States of America
Set in Garamond #3

Library of Congress Cataloging-in-Publication Data

Meltzer, Milton  Mary McLeod Bethune : voice of Black hope. (Women of our time) Originally
published: New York : Viking Kestrel, 1987. Summary: Traces the life and achievements of the black
educator who was instrumental in creating opportunities for blacks in education and government.
1. Bethune, Mary McLeod, 1875–1955—Childhood and youth—Juvenile literature. 2. Afro-
Americans—Biography—Juvenile literature.  3. Teachers—United States—Biography—Juvenile
literature.  [1. Bethune, Mary McLeod, 1875–1955.  2. Teachers.  3. Afro-American—
Biography]  I. Marchesi, Stephen, ill.  II. Title.  III. Series: Women of our time (Puffin Books)
E185.97.B34M45   1988      370′.092′4  [B]  [92]      87-25717
ISBN 0-14-032219-1

# CONTENTS

CHAPTER 1

Show Me an "A"   1

CHAPTER 2

Head, Heart and Hand   11

CHAPTER 3

A School of Her Own   21

CHAPTER 4

Better and Freer   32

CHAPTER 5

A New Deal   43

CHAPTER 6

Iron Fist, Velvet Glove   52

About This Book   58

# 1

## *Show Me an "A"*

That Saturday afternoon, Mary walked down the dusty road holding one end of the heavy laundry basket while her mother held the other. They were on their way to the Wilsons', with the clothes Mama washed for them every week. Mary was glad to help. With 17 children in the family, this was one of the rare times she had Mama all to herself.

When they came to the big house, Mama went in by the back door. You go visit with the children, she said. Mary found them in the yard, in the new playhouse. It was the first time she had seen the little house her father had just made for the daughters of

Ben Wilson, the white landowner he often did work for. The two little girls took her in and let her touch the dolls and even sit at one of the tiny desks. On it was a book, with the pages open. It had words printed in big black letters.

"Show me an 'A,' " Mary said. "Which one is it?"

"Put that book down," said the older girl. "You can't read! Come over here and I'll show you some pictures."

But pictures Mary could see for herself. She wanted to know how to read the words, how to make the letters tell her something. Slowly she closed the book and went over to look at the pictures. The Wilson girls could read, and they were no bigger than she was. Why could some people read and others not? "You can't read!" No, she couldn't. Neither could her mother and father, or her brothers and sisters. Nor any of the black folk she knew in their corner of South Carolina.

How come? she wondered on the way home. How come the white folks can read, and we can't? How come there's a school for them, but no school for us?

Mary Jane McLeod was born on July 10, 1875, in Mayesville, a country town in the midst of South Carolina's rice and cotton fields. The Civil War had ended only ten years before. Her mother, father and older brothers and sisters had been slaves until President Abraham Lincoln's Emancipation Proclamation. When Mary was born, the first free child in their own home after fourteen born in slavery, her mother said, "Thank God, Mary has come under our own vine and fig tree."

It was a family legend that Patsy McIntosh, Mary's mother, came of royal African blood. Small and delicate, she carried herself with quiet dignity. She could not read or write, but she spoke eloquently. And she had a great talent for organizing and planning. She grew up on a plantation close by the one Samuel McLeod was raised on. Their slaveowners had allowed them to marry. Samuel, a tall, sturdy farmer with skillful hands, was also an excellent carpenter and tinworker. Warmhearted and generous, he was a caring father.

After freedom came, the McLeods and their children earned wages for their labor. Over the years, they were able to save enough to buy five acres and then another thirty. Not content to live in an old slave hut, they cut wood and built a three-room log house of their own, placing it under a huge oak tree.

To the cabin, they added a porch and a kitchen. Out beyond was Patsy's wash shed.

The McLeods were a thrifty, hardworking family. In the nearby stream they fished for pike, mullet and eels, and in the woods they caught rabbits, possum

and quail. On the abandoned plantations nearby, the children gathered apples and peaches and dried them for winter storage.

But the core of their life was cotton. Mary's first memory was of the day her father swung her up on the high bristly back of Old Bush, the family mule. She was five then, old enough to help with the plowing. A smart girl like you, Samuel said, can keep the mule straight in the furrows. It'll speed up getting the cotton in the ground. Then he stepped back and took hold of the wooden handles of the plow.

Mary learned to measure time not by hours or days but by planting time, chopping time and picking time. You put the cotton seed into the plowed earth when the weather was right. When the weeds came up among the cotton stalks, you got out into the hot sun with a hoe and chopped them down. And when the fat white bolls burst miraculously into rich bloom, you ran into the fields to pick the blobs of white stuff at feverish speed. By the age of nine, Mary could pick 250 pounds of cotton a day. Back bent, dragging a burlap sack over her left shoulder, working with both hands, she would snap off cotton bolls till her hands were full and then reach back and drop them into the sack.

If the crop was good, and the market right, the McLeods could hope for a fair price. When they sold their crop, they could pay their debts, buy supplies and maybe have a few dollars for fun. Mostly fun made by themselves. It was a time long before radio and television and movies and recordings. The neighbors got together at certain seasons of the year for pleasure or to help each other. There were cotton pickings and corn huskings and fodder strippings and sometimes hog killings. When the task was finished, there would be eats and drinks and dancing in the moonlight.

Many of Mary's brothers and sisters had married and left home before she was born. When she was growing up, there were seven or eight children still around. Her mother worked in the fields as well as doing washing or cooking or other chores for white people. Sometimes she was called out in the night to hurry to some neighbor's cabin to midwife the birth of a new baby. Each of her children had a task to do, acccording to what they were best at. And they knew, from the way Samuel and Patsy did things, that no matter what your job, you must do it right. Some milked the cow, others helped with the washing, ironing, cooking, housecleaning. Her father said Mary was his champion cotton-picker.

The only one who didn't work any longer was Patsy's mother, Granny Sophia. Except for brewing medicines from the root herbs the children gathered in the swamp. She was ancient now, wrinkled and toothless, her white hair always bound in a red bandanna.

She liked to sit close to the fire's warmth, rocking gently, murmuring, or singing quietly to herself. When Mary finished her chores in the evening, she would come sit on a footstool by Granny's rocker. The old lady often praised God for letting her live out her years in freedom, in a loving family, where she could taste hot biscuits with butter, and coffee with cream.

Granny's own mother, she told Mary, had been raised in an African village. Her people herded cattle and grew crops. One day, when the grain was ripening, slavers raided the village and carried Granny's mother off in chains. She was brought across the Atlantic in a slave ship and sold to a rice planter in South Carolina. Granny made life in Africa real for Mary, telling her stories she had heard from Mary's great-grandmother. Old as she was, Granny never forgot who she was, and where she came from, and Mary grew up proud of her African heritage.

For the McLeods, the Fourth of July was a very special day. Not only because it marked the birth of the nation. But because sister Sallie had been born on the fourth, Mary on the tenth and Hattie on the twelfth. So Independence Day became a day of family reunion, with a big dinner set out on a long table under the oak tree and mother, father, children and grandchildren celebrating freedom.

Once, when Mary's birthday fell on a Saturday, her

father took her to market with him in Mayesville. As they were watching the sale of horses and mules at the fairground, Mary saw a drunken white man shove a flaming match into a black man's face. When the black man flung out his arm to avoid being burned, he struck the white man. Other whites standing nearby grabbed the black man and yelled for a rope to "String him up!" Terrified, Mary cried "Papa! Papa!" and tugged at him to get her out of this crazed mob. He snatched her up and ordering her not to look back, raced for their mule and wagon. On the way home, he was silent and grim. When they reached the cabin, he started to tell Patsy about the lynching. But she put her hand over his mouth and told the children to go to bed.

Huddling under the quilt, Mary could hear the murmur of their voices. She squinched her eyes tight to blot out the picture of the enraged whites dragging the frightened black man toward a tree. It was hours before she fell asleep.

She took comfort from the strength of her father and mother. They held family prayers every morning and evening, and on Sundays the family traveled five miles to Mayesville for services at the Methodist Episcopal Church. They could not read the prayer books, but the words of the preacher and the music of the choir spoke to their minds and hearts. In bed at night, Mary could often hear her mother, on the other side of the wall, praying for love, for knowledge, for strength, for the good things of life not only for her family but for all the poor and oppressed.

Mary did not look like either of her parents. Her face was broad, her body squarely built, her skin blue-black, her eyes hazel-brown. Her hands were shaped like her mother's, and she had the manual skills of both Samuel and Patsy. She could cook and crochet with the best, as well as chop and pick cotton like a champion.

Early on, the family and neighbors sensed that little Mary was somehow different. Her mind was quick, her thoughts deep. The neighbors believed that when Mary was born, her eyes were wide open. The midwife who delivered her, it is said, told Mary's mother that her baby would always see things before they happened. As things turned out, sometimes she did predict what would happen. Was it a gift, or just that she understood the movement of history? She did have a great gift of the tongue. She talked as fluently as her mother and loved to argue any question. While both parents enjoyed music, Mary's talent for singing came from her father. She learned the old slave songs and spirituals from him. When neighbors joined them in field labor, they always did best when they heard young Mary's voice sing out "Ev'ry time I feel de spirit, movin' in my heart."

10

# 2

## *Head, Heart and Hand*

Cotton, cotton, cotton.

Season after season.

Mary worked hard, but while she worked, the fever to read never died away. She prayed to the Lord to help her find a path to schooling. But in those days how could a black child, especially in the South, get an education? For hundreds of miles around, there was not a single school for blacks. And black children were not allowed in public schools with white children.

One day someone knocked on the cabin door. There stood a young black woman, dressed in city clothes. She was Miss Emma Wilson, sent by the Northern Presbyterian Church to start a mission school for blacks in nearby Mayesville. Would you like to send any of your children? she asked Samuel and Patsy. They didn't need to stop and think. Mary, they said, Mary is the one. They would have liked to send them all, but they could hardly spare even one for all the farm labor that needed to be done. Mary must go; she was special.

"It changed my life overnight," Mary wrote years later. Every morning, wearing her new shoes with copper toes, her sunbonnet and shawl, she picked up her little lunch pail of bread and milk and walked five miles to school; every afternoon, five miles home. School was held for only four months of the year, in between the cotton seasons.

The school was in a small shack in the black neighborhood of Mayesville. It was one of many mission schools opened by northern churches to reach into places where public schools had never come. A year or so later, money was found to build a two-room yellow brick schoolhouse.

That first day, Miss Wilson opened the Bible to John 3:16 and read: "For God so loved the world, that He gave His only begotten Son, that whosoever believeth in him should not perish, but have ever-lasting life."

With those words, Mary recalled, "the scales fell from my eyes, and the light came flooding in. My sense of inferiority, my fear of handicaps, dropped away. Whosoever, it said. No Jew nor Gentile, no Catholic nor Protestant, no black nor white; just 'whosoever.' It meant that I, a humble Negro girl, had just as much chance as anybody in the sight and love of God. These words stored up a battery of faith and confidence and determination in my heart, which has not failed me to this day. . . ."

From Miss Emma, Mary learned the ABCs. She mastered reading and writing and arithmetic. She learned something of history and geography and, of course, Bible studies. The classroom had old second-hand desks and chairs, a cracked blackboard, a pot-bellied stove that filled the air with smoke on chilly days. But the children decorated the school with cut-out paper flowers, pasted their artwork on the walls and hung rope swings on the trees in the yard.

Mary was one of the hardest-working students. She quickly put her learning to use every way she could. She stood by her father at the cotton gin when the white man weighed the McLeod bales, and calculated what the price should be. There was no more cheating. And she made sure the figures were right when her father paid the bills he owed the white merchants.

As soon as she understood something new in school, she rushed back to teach it to the others at home. Miss Wilson had been sent a box of small Bibles and other texts. She gave Mary one of each to keep, and Mary read aloud from them to her proud family circle.

Early on, like her mother, she showed a gift for organizing. She got the neighbors' children to join in a Tin Can Banking Circle, putting aside pennies they earned selling berries or plums. Then when Christmas came, they all had something to spend for gifts. She organized a Mouth Organ Band, too, which played music for the children and grown-ups to dance by.

She stayed four years at the mission school. She learned everything it had to teach. At graduation, she put on the first white dress she had ever worn. She was eleven now. But she knew her education wasn't finished. She had more to learn, much more. But where? How? When?

She went back home to do the farm and household chores she had always done. A year passed, with Mary praying in the cotton fields for another chance to go on with her schooling.

Then way off in Colorado, a schoolteacher answered her prayer. Miss Mary Chrissman had been getting leaflets sent out by the Presbyterian Mission Board. Miss Chrissman was a Quaker who faithfully gave a portion of her earnings to carry on work that would make people's lives a little better. She read in a leaflet about the school for blacks in Mayesville. She wrote to ask if she could help one child in Miss Wilson's school who would benefit from higher education. She pledged to pay the tuition out of her extra earnings as a seamstress.

Miss Wilson replied she knew just the right student for her generous gift—Mary McLeod. And the right school for her to go to—Scotia, a seminary. It was for black girls at Concord, North Carolina, and it had been her own school. The news of Mary's great luck electrified the community. Not only her family but the neighbors gave stockings and a dress and a sweater and shoes to prepare Mary for what she felt was a journey to heaven.

In the fall of 1887, she boarded a train—her first train ride ever—for the school in North Carolina. Scotia was a three-story brick building standing on a small campus with green lawns and bright flowers. Mary was assigned to room with a girl who'd been there a year. Abbie Greeley—who became her best friend—explained the school routine, showed her where everything was, eased her into a new life.

Some of Scotia's dozen teachers were black, and some white. Mary saw how they helped one another, working together as equals. She had never met either

whites or blacks as educated as these men and women were. Later she said:

*The white teachers taught that the color of a person's skin has nothing to do with his brains, and that color, caste, or class distinctions are an evil thing. . . . I can never doubt the sincerity and wholeheartedness of some white people when I remember my experience with these beloved, consecrated teachers who took so much time and patience with me. . . .*

Make something of everything you have, was the school's guiding principle. Head, heart, hand are equally important. Learn to use them together.

And Mary tried her best. She did well in some studies, only fair in others. She had trouble with algebra and geometry, but mastered Latin grammar. Although her penmanship was poor, the English compositions she wrote were excellent. In geography and history she got decent grades. Music—that was where she shone, with her superb voice and her joy in using it. She proved how wrong was the common belief of whites that black people were inferior and unfit for education.

Students who could afford it paid tuition, but all were given work to do. Mary waited on table, helped in the kitchen, cleaned the halls, sorted the laundry, scrubbed the stairs. Between terms, she earned money by working for white families at their summer homes. She was a baby-sitter, a laundress, a housecleaner, a dairy maid. Such experience added much to her education. Later, when she created a school of her own, it proved invaluable.

Twice, little as she could spare the money, Mary went home to see her family. She found Granny barely clinging to the last shred of life. Was her mother always so small and so frail? And her father—he had sunk into silence under the weight of his troubles. Paying off the last dollars he owed on the mule meant they'd gone hungry. And the hooded Klansmen—a terrorist group that hated blacks—were still marching and burning crosses in the vain attempt to stop Mr. McLeod from voting. Young friends she'd grown up with were deserting the South in the hope of making a better life in the West.

By now Mary was one of the most popular girls at Scotia. And a leader the students turned to when they needed someone to speak for them. Mary helped straighten out their personal difficulties with the teachers, she got the dining hall to provide more variety in the meals and the president to ease up on strict rules of behavior. She learned how to deal calmly with others and work out reasonable settlement of her differences with them. As president of the literary society and member of the debating team, she developed great skill in leading discussions and chairing meetings.

In 1890, she advanced to Scotia's Normal School, where she practiced the art of teaching. All these years she wrote regularly to Miss Chrissman, her sponsor in Colorado. She sent her lively reports on her progress and voiced her gratitude for the chance she had given Mary.

In July 1894, Mary graduated from Scotia. Nobody came from home to see her get her diploma. The train fare was more than they could earn in many months. But she was surrounded by affectionate classmates and teachers. And now, Miss Chrissman was giving her another chance—this time for a year's study in Chicago. It would prepare her to do mission work in Africa. At Scotia she had heard visiting missionaries talk about saving souls in Africa. They seemed to think Africa was full of savages who had no history. But Mary knew better; she remembered stories Granny had told her.

A week after graduation, Mary caught the train to Chicago. She looked very different from the backwoods girl who had arrived seven years before. She wore a white blouse, a long blue skirt, high, laced shoes, white gloves and a white straw sailor hat.

She entered the Mission Training School of Moody Bible Institute just as she turned nineteen. There were

about one thousand students there; she was the only black. The students were sent out to carry the Gospel into the slums of Chicago. They sang on the street, handed out leaflets, urged people to come to the weekly services. Mary sang in the school chorus. When her pure soprano pierced through the other voices, they made her a soloist. She helped to establish Sunday schools in the Midwest, traveling aboard a Gospel train.

When the year was over, she applied to the Mission Board for assignment to Africa. That was what they had trained her for. Yet she was refused. They said there were no openings for black missionaries—in black Africa!

# 3

## *A School of Her Own*

To be turned down was a bitter disappointment. The mission school was prejudiced against blacks when it came to finding them work. Mary decided to go home and give back something of what she had been given. She would help Miss Wilson teach the twenty children in the mission school at Mayesville where she had started. The first day of school, she watched the children come in from the yard. Now *she* was the teacher— to be called "Miss" or "Mrs." for the first time. And till the end of her life. She would never doubt this was what she was born to do.

The year went well. But though her county needed many teachers, there was hardly enough money for Miss Wilson. So Mary wrote the Board of Missions asking to be sent to another school. Soon she heard from Haines Institute in Augusta, Georgia, offering her a post teaching the eighth grade.

Haines was headed by Lucy C. Laney. Born in slavery, she had made herself a pioneer educator. Ten years before, she had opened her private school for black children in the basement of a church. Georgia had no black high schools and few elementary schools. Blacks were fit only for menial jobs, said most educators. But Miss Laney did not agree. She helped her pupils stretch to their full capacity as human beings.

"From Miss Laney," Mary said, "I got a new vision: my life work lay not in Africa but in my own country." One day she would have a school of her own.

After a year at Haines, the Mission Board sent Mary to teach at Kindell Institute in Sumter, Georgia. Mary lived as cheaply as possible and sent home most of her earnings to pay off her father's mortgage. She sang with the church choir, where she met a young man with a tenor voice that blended beautifully with hers. Albertus Bethune taught Mary to ride a bicycle and they went on long trips into the countryside. When they fell in love, she took Albertus home to meet her family. In May of 1898, when Mary was twenty-three, they were married. They moved to Savannah because Albertus had found a job there selling men's clothing. In 1899, their son Albert was born—the ninetieth grandchild of Samuel and Patsy.

Mary gave up teaching for a while so "I could be all mother for one precious year. After that I got restless again to be back at my beloved work, for having a child made me more than ever determined to build better lives for my people."

She went back to teaching when she was asked to take charge of a new mission school in Palatka, a small town in Florida on the St. Johns River. Albertus was not eager to go along. So she went on ahead, with her husband hoping she'd get discouraged soon and come back.

She rented a cottage in Palatka and found an old friend willing to take care of her baby during school hours. Soon Albertus decided to join her, although he did not have much faith in her plans.

Busy as she was, she reached out into the community. She helped the black people in the overcrowded neighborhoods they were confined to, and visited the prisoners in the county jail. She liked teaching as much as ever, but if only she had a school of her own. . . .

She was at Palatka for nearly four years when, one night in a dream, she saw a great assembly of boys and girls, the girls in white blouses and blue skirts, the boys in dark suits. There seemed to be thousands of them, standing, waiting, for whom? for what? She woke in wild excitement. Did it mean she must go on from here, to find the young people who needed her?

Every day now, she saw families of black people from Alabama and Georgia and the Carolinas passing through Palatka in their wagons loaded with pots and pans and clothing and bedding. They camped overnight on the riverbank and in the morning, headed deeper south. Where you bound for? she asked. It was jobs they were after, building a railroad down the east coast of Florida into the new vacationland the rich were flocking to.

Maybe this was where she was needed. With hundreds of workers and their children moving into the railroad construction camps, surely they'd need a school and community services. The Reverend S. P. Pratt, a Baptist minister who knew of her yearning for a school of her own, suggested Daytona Beach as the place to go. It was fifty miles south of Palatka, and a thriving tourist town with elegant hotels. Many rich people had recently built handsome winter homes there. Wealthy whites were the ones who had given money to Lucy Laney's school. Why couldn't Mary reach them with the same appeal for help?

She would see for herself. She took the train south

to Daytona Beach and looked up Mrs. Susie Warren, a friend of the Reverend Mr. Pratt. Mrs. Warren had three girls who went to a small public school for blacks open only three months of the year. She'd like a better school for them. And so would others. A hopeful sign was the kindergarten that wealthy white women had opened for the children of the blacks who worked for them. Perhaps she could get these women to support her school.

The black section of Daytona Beach was full of shacks, and the people had no running water, but the unpaved streets were lined with tall palms and great oaks. Here Mary found a shabby four-room cottage the owner said he'd rent as a school for eleven dollars a month. She had only a dollar and a half in cash. He took it on the pledge she'd pay the rest by the end of the month.

That was September 1904. She stayed on at Mrs. Warren's and plunged into creating a school out of nothing. Ministers let her speak to their congregations and ask for help. She begged stores for boxes to use as chairs and cut a barrel in half for her own seat. To every woman she met she talked school, school, school.

On October 3, 1904, she opened the door of what she grandly named the Daytona Literary and Industrial School for Training Negro Girls. Five little girls showed up, aged 8 to 12. They were Anne, Celeste,

Lena, Lucille and Ruth. Their parents paid Mary 50 cents a week for tuition. Her own son, now five, was the only boy in The School, as it was quickly called by everyone. "Though I hadn't a penny left," Mary said, "I considered cash money as the smallest part of my resources. I had faith in a living God, faith in myself, and a desire to serve."

She burned logs and used the charred splinters as pencils. She mashed elderberries for ink. She made a packing case into her desk. Very soon her pupils increased. Mothers who were maids had to go off for a season with the white families they worked for. They left their small children with the school. Mary found cast-off beds, cleaned and painted them, sewed together corn sacks for mattresses and stuffed them with dried Spanish moss. The neighbors answered generously to her calls for help. Fishermen shared a good catch with her. Volunteers ran chicken suppers and gave the small profits to buy food. Mary baked sweet potato pies she sold to the railroad workers. Somehow she scraped together enough to meet each month's rent and the grocery bills.

Curious neighbors dropped in to look over the school. When she found they couldn't read or write she offered to start evening classes. Those who could, paid her a dollar a week and the others did odd jobs around the school. She saw the need to help married couples and formed a special group for them. She showed them ways to improve their housekeeping, to manage on their low incomes, to care for their children.

Sunday afternoons became Open House time, with everyone welcome. Mary would give a short talk on black history, building their pride in who their people were and what they had done. She formed a quartet with herself and Albertus and two other good voices. They sang folk songs and spirituals and then everyone—children and adults—joined in. Albertus liked the singing, but he didn't think Mary's hard work would add up to anything.

Black coachmen would drive their carriages past

the school on Sunday afternoons so their white employers would hear the music in the air. Captivated by the rich sound, the sightseers would stop and Mary would welcome them in. She never let up trying to enlarge the ever-growing circle of white supporters. She printed leaflets about the school and handed them out in the business district. She knocked on doors, she wrote letters, she gave talks to any group that would listen. From every corner of Florida came applications from black parents eager to send their girls. Some could not pay; instead they sent chickens and eggs and hams. She took over a big barn nearby and fixed it up for a dormitory. Her girls ransacked Daytona's junkyards to find dishes and pots and furniture that could still be made useful.

It wasn't enough. In two years, her school had grown from 5 to 250 students. She had to put up a new building to meet the need. She found the spot—a dump called Hell's Hole on the edge of the black district. It was bordered by towering oaks, and she knew she could transform this wasteland into a garden. The price was $250. She talked the owner into taking $5 down and the rest within two years. She didn't even have the $5; she raised it by selling ice cream and sweet potato pies.

That's how the Bethune-Cookman College campus started.

Every day, her girls came down to the dump to reduce the mound of rubbish. They carted off the junk bit by bit. The leveled site was at last ready for construction work. But where was the money?

In her night school were gardeners and caretakers and coachmen from the estates on the beach. They told their bosses about what Mary was trying to do, and gave her hints on how to approach them. She started with James Gamble, head of the huge corporation, Procter & Gamble. His gardener said he was a "real kind man." She wrote to ask if he could see her. Yes, he replied, tomorrow at one. She bicycled over, thinking how best to awaken his interest. She didn't need to rehearse the words; they always came easily to her.

She told Mr. Gamble about the school and asked him to visit it. He came the next day and inspected everything carefully. He agreed to be a trustee, and gave her a check for $150. For many years, he would be one of the school's most generous friends. Mary built on that beginning and soon had the mayor, prominent local businessmen, black ministers and other wealthy winter residents sitting down together as trustees to plan The School's development. She believed strongly in interracial cooperation, and succeeded in getting black and white people to work together.

One day a stranger came to see the school. He said his name was Thomas H. White, but it meant nothing to her. He looked around, saw the unfinished new building. Construction had stopped till more funds could be raised. Then he entered a room where the dressmaking class was working with an ancient Singer sewing machine. He turned to Mary and said, "I believe you are on the right track. This is the most promising thing I've seen in Florida." He wrote out a check and left. It was for $250. The next day he came back, with a new sewing machine. Only then did Mary learn that Mr. White was Singer's chief competitor.

Again and again he returned—with painters, plasterers, carpenters, masons and materials to finish the new building. She named it Faith Hall. He brought blankets for the children, shoes and a coat for Mary, everything they had dreamed of having someday. When she thanked him in tears, he waved her aside. "I've never invested a dollar that has brought greater returns than the dollars I have given you," he said. When he died, he left the school a trust fund of $67,000.

No wonder Mary had faith. "I never stop to plan," she said. "I take things step by step. We have never had to close our doors for lack of food or fuel, although often we have to live from day to day."

# 4

## *Better and Freer*

One morning, a student felt terrible pain in her stomach and ran a high fever. Mary thought it must be appendicitis. There were no hospitals for blacks in Daytona. Mary bicycled to the local hospital and begged a white doctor to take the child and operate. He finally agreed. Soon after the surgery she visited her pupil:

"When I appeared at the front door of the hospital the nurse ordered me around to the back way. I thrust her aside—and found my little girl segregated in a corner of the porch behind the kitchen. Even my toes clenched with rage.

"That decided me. I called on three of my faithful friends, asking them to buy a little cottage behind our school as a hospital. They agreed, and we started with two beds."

From that small beginning grew a fully equipped 20-bed hospital. It was not only for the school, but for sick blacks throughout the state. It was staffed by black and white doctors and by the school's own student nurses. McLeod Hospital (she named it in honor of her parents) ran for twenty years as part of the school's contribution to community life; then the city took it over.

It was typical of Mary's way. Whenever she saw a need for some training or service, she added it to the school's program. She opened the school library to all, making it the only place in the state where a black boy or girl could find free books to read.

From the black educator Booker T. Washington she picked up the idea of holding community conferences. She organized a countywide conference where prizes were given for the best vegetables, jellies, needlework. The women met to exchange ideas on baby care and child-rearing and household management. Soon the idea spread to three counties, with everyone striving to develop healthier children, more attractive homes and better gardens.

To the school itself she added a small farm, at first

only twelve acres. She had the students work in the garden before or after classroom sessions. Later the students raised chickens, hogs and cattle. The school gave away food to neighbors in need of it. The farm became a model for the community, its products displayed and sold together with handicrafts at an annual bazaar.

But she did more than work toward helping her people to live better. She tried to help them to live freer. She opened the school three nights a week for adult classes in the three Rs and in civics. By civics she meant learning about your civil rights and how to use them. People found out why it was so important to pay your poll tax—even if you went hungry—so that you could register and vote for what you needed and what you believed in. All who came to those night classes went out to use their constitutional rights. Well before women had won the right to vote, in 1920, Mary had made herself a political power in the community.

Of course, it wasn't enough to make a radical improvement in black life. This was the early 1900s, when the black was no longer a slave, and yet not a full citizen. Everywhere blacks turned, they saw signs telling them FOR WHITES ONLY. They couldn't live where they liked, eat where they liked, play where they liked, buy where they liked, work where they liked. The people who held the power clung to their old belief that whites were better than blacks. Even when factories were built in the South, their doors were closed to blacks. They were left in their old role of tenant farmer, common laborer and household servant. The new cotton mills were staffed by whites and the towns run by the companies were fortresses of segregation. Only whites could live in them.

The public schools, too, were segregated—separate schools for whites and for blacks. And the money and attention given to black schools lagged far behind the white. For every tax dollar spent on buildings and teachers and books and supplies for whites, only 20 cents was spent on blacks.

Violence against blacks exploded often on the nation's front pages. In the first decades of the 1900s, terrible race riots broke out. Mobs of furious whites swept through the streets of several cities, beating and killing the blacks they met. And thousands of lynchings took place not only in the South but in many parts of the North.

Against this setting, Mary Bethune's struggle for decent education and equality appears heroic. She knew the facts of black life. She wanted to train her students to work for a living at all the jobs in town or country that might be open to them. But she wanted to inspire those with special ability to move on to

higher studies. She strengthened in her students the desire to make the world a better place to live.

By 1914, Mary was offering a full high-school program with special training in teaching, nursing, cooking and homemaking. There had been only one high school in Florida for blacks until them. Now a much bigger building than Faith Hall went up. Over the main entrance was inscribed, ENTER TO LEARN, and inside, as students left, they saw the words, DEPART TO SERVE.

She was able to add two years of college work and to pay salaries to teachers sent out to the workers in the turpentine camps nearby. Because she kept the tuition low, she had to work all the harder to raise money to meet the school's expenses. She had taken in a few boys by this time, and wanted to add more. But that meant more buildings, workshops, teachers. She solved the problem by combining her school with the Cookman Institute for boys in Jacksonville. The coeducational school was named Bethune-Cookman College, and she became its first president. It grew rapidly. As needs changed, the elementary and high-school sections were dropped. The school became a standard junior college with an A rating.

Mrs. Bethune was now middle-aged. She had earned her place as an American leader of national influence. She had become heavier in figure, and her jet-black hair showed streaks of white. But her energy seemed limitless. Her personal life had suffered painful changes. Her parents were gone. Her marriage had ended by divorce long before. She and Albertus saw things too differently for a marriage to succeed.

While Mrs. Bethune always stood for black freedom, she did not neglect the fight for the rights of women. They, too, had been denied their place as American citizens. Women—black or white—still did not have the right to vote. For more than fifty years now they had pressed Congress to adopt a constitutional amendment to guarantee that "No citizen shall be deprived of the right to vote because of sex." Black women had joined with white in the campaign, working through their own organizations. Mrs. Bethune was active in the Equal Suffrage League, formed by the National Association of Colored Women.

After the First World War, Congress finally passed the Nineteenth Amendment, assuring women the right to vote. So women now had the chance to cast their ballots for candidates they hoped would make laws to improve their lives.

The chance—if white politicians would not stand in the way. She knew from bitter experience how often laws in the past had been ignored or defied. One trick used was the poll tax. It cost each voter $1.50, a lot for people who earned so little. Mrs. Bethune walked through the black neighborhoods to urge people to make every sacrifice to vote.

On the night before the election, eighty white-robed horsemen of the Ku Klux Klan rode up to the school, their torches flaring in the dark. Everyone knew the Klan was guilty of torture and murder, but almost never was punished. Warned that they might come, Mrs. Bethune had every light in the school turned on, to show her defiance. The hooded Klan leaders came up to Mrs. Bethune, standing alone on the steps. They threatened to burn the place down if she kept on rallying black people to vote. If you burn down our school, she replied, we will rebuild it again, and again and again. From behind, floating out the windows, came the voices of the school choir, singing "My Soul Is Anchored in the Lord; No Man Can Harm Me." Slowly the masked men turned and rode away, leaving their kerosene can on the ground.

The next morning, Mrs. Bethune proudly led a procession of black voters through the streets and into the voting booths to cast their ballots for democracy.

The story of her courage spread far and wide. She had long been a popular speaker on behalf of the school. Now she was invited to meetings and conferences to have her say whenever black rights and needs were discussed. She was earnest and eloquent; her words opened minds and touched hearts.

She never came back from those meetings without new ideas for action. As soon as she saw a need, she began to think of a way to fill it. "I pray to God," she'd say, "to let me do something about it." She joined two new organizations that *were* doing something—the National Urban League and the National Association for the Advancement of Colored People. The first tried to open up more and better jobs for blacks, and to improve their housing conditions. The brilliant lawyers of the second group fought segregation and discrimination through the courts.

But the problems closest to Mrs. Bethune's heart were those of the South. She loved her beautiful homeland; why couldn't it offer hope to the black and the poor? Millions suffered in the South. If only she could rouse them to change their lives. She came to believe that women were the key to change. Who knew the problems, the pain, the cost better than they? Hadn't her grandmother and her mother resisted and survived the horrors of slavery? "We shall find a way to do for our day what they did for theirs," she said.

Scattered through the South were hundreds of small clubs of black women, brave women who worked for change. She was determined to bring their lonely efforts together into one great organization to fight for justice. There was a National Association of Colored

Women, but all its members lived in the North and the West. Her job would be to bring the voice and the power of the black women of her region, the South, into the association.

She began by pulling together the Florida clubs, then she created a southeastern regional organization. And in 1924 she became president of the national organization. It was the highest office open to a black woman in that time. In that position of leadership, she inspired black women to greater heights of service. Her faith in them and what they could do was limitless. "Next to God," she once said, "we are indebted to women, first for life itself, and then for making it worth having." Everywhere Mrs. Bethune traveled, her ideas, her personality, her achievements helped whites to understand what black women had done and could yet do.

In the 1930s Mrs. Bethune created the National Council of Negro Women. It united the major national black women's associations and became the strong central voice its 800,000 members needed. She served as its president for 14 years. She knew when to praise and when to push, always working to get groups to agree on common action. She led the campaigns against segregation and discrimination.

All this, while continuing to head the college she founded.

# 5

---

# *A New Deal*

It looked as if Mrs. Bethune would never find time for the lighter side of life. True, she took pleasure in her work. She enjoyed her friendships and her ties with her students and staff. Sometimes those friendships were troubled by the very strength of her personality. The people around her could feel overpowered. Yet she had a great ability to shake people out of their ruts and spur them to do more than they thought they could.

Traveling about the country for the school, she liked to sing for her audiences and used her even greater talent as a public speaker to tell them the story of her life. She made a handsome figure on the platform. She never forgot the early days when her clothes came out of missionary barrels, and now she delighted in smart dresses set off by a pearl necklace. She was fond of other jewelry, too, and chose her earrings, bracelets and rings carefully.

But she had never gone abroad. Some friends plotted to get her to accept an eight-week trip to Europe. She had an audience with the pope in Rome, she dined with the lord mayor of London, and in Paris, she met with distinguished African scholars. She charmed the men she met and one even proposed marriage to her. At Monte Carlo, she marveled at the people she saw gambling feverishly. She went mountain climbing in Switzerland, using an alpenstock to help, and always after that kept a cane to wave about just for the fun of it. Sailing home, her ship met a heavy storm and Mrs. Bethune cheerfully advised the captain how to get through it safely.

Not long after she returned home, the Great Depression hit America. By the winter of 1932, there were 15 million people out of work. Homeless men and women were sleeping in subways and the hungry were begging on the streets. Breadlines and soup kitchens were everywhere. A huge army of Americans drifted across the country in search of work. Many of them were boys and girls. They rode in freight cars, slept in hobo jungles, died of disease and exposure and lack of food.

Mrs. Bethune felt the Depression slam into Florida like a hurricane. The tourist trade collapsed. Black men begged for odd jobs at any wages and found none. Their wives cooked in white kitchens for 50 cents a week or just for the leftovers they could bring to their hungry families. Although Bethune-Cookman College cut its tuition fee, many students had to drop out. Mrs. Bethune stopped her own salary and struggled to keep paying her staff. She raised more food on the campus farm to save her students from hunger.

She held out her hand to anyone who needed help. Once a young black struggling to make a living as a writer in those grim thirties stopped by to see her college. It was Langston Hughes. He had published poems and books. They had earned him a reputation, not money. He had heard this college would permit no segregation; whites who came by to hear music or a lecture had to sit with blacks. He admired what it took to defy law and custom and wanted to meet the lady who had guts.

Mrs. Bethune welcomed him warmly with a room and a good meal. The next day, she had him read his poems to her English classes. That night, she sat up late with him to talk. She could feel he was drifting, uncertain, unable to realize the goal he had set—to be a writer and make a living at it. In her wisdom she said, but you've found the way, only you don't realize it! She reminded him how eagerly the students had listened to him, how proud they were that a young black poet had made a mark in American literature. Don't you see, she said, that you make them feel they, too, can achieve something in this world—in spite of the color line?

It changed his life. Now he saw that if he planned tours of schools and colleges and churches and lodges, reading his poems to black audiences for a fee, and added that income to whatever his writing might bring in, he could make a decent living. "This is what you have to do," Mrs. Bethune said. "People need poetry."

They needed bread, too. But for a long time, nothing was done for the hungry because the government and business refused to face the truth. They believed the country was "basically sound," and the trouble would work itself out. But it didn't. One winter, two winters, three winters of depression went by.

For blacks, life had been hard long before the Great Depression. But when it came, blacks suffered even more than whites. By 1932, one out of every two black adults was jobless. It is hard to imagine what that meant in misery and hopelessness.

In the South, the Depression made what had never

been a good life even worse. The South was the poorest part of the country. It was at the bottom in health, housing, education, jobs, wages. And at the bottom of the bottom, thought Mrs. Bethune, are my people.

Then a new president was elected by a people desperate for action. Although born into wealth, Franklin D. Roosevelt had been made a cripple for life by polio. He recognized that society had an obligation to the poor, the sick, the helpless. He felt badly for the victims of the Depression and wanted to help. Under a bleak gray sky in March 1933, Roosevelt took the oath of office. "The only thing we have to fear is fear itself," he said.

He used his power to wage war against the emergency. Congress passed bill after bill to create jobs for the unemployed by spending billions for badly needed public works—hospitals, schools, community centers, playgounds, roads, bridges, dams. Farmers were helped, wages and hours were improved, relief was provided for the needy, low-cost public housing was launched, conservation camps took homeless boys off city streets.

For blacks, the New Deal, as FDR's program was called, made a great difference. Segregation and discrimination continued, despite rules against it. But a great many got jobs, and better pay than before. And with federal help, black farmers were able to buy land.

No one knew better than Mrs. Bethune what the needs of young blacks were. "The drums of Africa beat in my heart," she would often say. "I cannot rest while there is a single Negro boy or girl lacking the chance to prove his worth." In 1935 her great experience and skills were recognized in Washington. She had come to know the president's wife, Eleanor Roosevelt, many years earlier. As they had worked together on several racial issues, Mrs. Roosevelt had learned to overcome the prejudice within herself. She became a believer in Mrs. Bethune, and everything she stood for. Mrs. Bethune can be useful, she said to the head of the National Youth Administration. So he appointed Mrs. Bethune to be an adviser to the NYA. Its primary aim was to help young people between sixteen and twenty-four to find part-time work.

Mrs. Bethune's job was to give advice. She had no power, no pay and no prestige in this remote corner of government. But it was not in her nature to be ignored. She settled into a small apartment in the capital and went to work. She gathered around her many young people, black and white, who had flooded into the capital to help make the New Deal a success. They talked with her day and night, debating ideas for new projects and new approaches. This was the future they were planning: it was a great chance to make progress. What direction should the country take? How far could blacks go in the face of ancient prejudices?

Within a year, everyone in Washington knew a major force had come to town. Mrs. Bethune was put in charge of black affairs within the NYA. Now she had a salary and authority. She made herself the heart of this great effort to realize the vision of equal justice. It was a rare time to be in the center of action. And she enjoyed it. There are many photographs of her in these years. Though only five feet six inches tall, she looks majestic. This is me! she seems to be saying to the camera, proud and beautiful.

The young people she worked with called her Mother. She gave them her support, her confidence, her strength. They became like sons and daughters to her. She did not limit her concern to the NYA. She boldly assumed the role of spokesperson to the government for all black people. They had long viewed her as a great leader: she understood their dreams and hopes and problems. They knew she could speak for them.

But to do that most effectively she needed solid support. Each of the federal agencies had black advisers. Working separately they could do much less than working together. So just as she had got black women to work cooperatively, she now organized the Federal Council on Negro Affairs. It was an informal group of blacks in government that soon became known as the Black Cabinet. They met weekly in Mrs. Bethune's home. They attacked discrimination in government facilities. They fought for greater opportunities for blacks in government jobs. They tried to stop government actions that might harm blacks.

Through their efforts, the press gave more attention to the role of government in meeting black interests. Two national black conferences Mrs. Bethune organized were widely reported and made the whole nation aware of the problems of blacks and what they wanted done to solve them.

With such strong support, Mrs. Bethune often went directly to the president and Mrs. Roosevelt to urge them to advance civil rights and promote black concerns. Once the president said of her, "Mrs. Bethune is a great woman. I believe in her because she has her feet on the ground—not only on the ground but in the deep, plowed soil." She went beyond the bounds of government to carry on the fight. She picketed businesses in Washington that refused to hire blacks. She demonstrated to gain the right to organize for black sharecroppers in the South. She spoke at rallies of many civil rights organizations. Hers was a down-

home style that audiences liked: "You white folks have long been eating the white meat of the chicken," she'd say. "We Negroes are now ready for some of the white meat instead of the dark."

# 6

## *Iron Fist, Velvet Glove*

Mrs. Bethune was a great power for good in her ten years in Washington. She knew how to lead people, and she understood what could be done at that time in history. She pushed the government to give black people their due, and showed her anger when officials, even the highest, failed to move. She insisted on the right of blacks to make their own decisions. "The white man has been thinking for us too long," she said. "We want him to think with us instead of for us."

She had her weaknesses, of course. She tried to do

too much herself, failing to give others authority, holding too many strings in her own hands.

Now in her sixties, she suffered from asthma, and was overweight, too. Even so, she could travel 40,000 miles through 21 states in one year, speak at 40 meetings and see what else the NYA could do to help black youth. Over 600,000 of them benefited from the NYA. They cleared parks and playgrounds, built dormitories and classrooms, repaired roads, planted trees. Those in school learned trades in exchange for board and tuition. It made them proud.

Whenever the Congress threatened to cut NYA's budget, she hurried to the president and Mrs. Roosevelt to gain their support for full funding. The southern states stubbornly refused to appoint black NYA advisers. She lobbied to change that and soon had blacks appointed in every state but Mississippi. She set up resident training programs of the NYA in many black colleges. She got a hundred librarians added to black universities and had the NYA train high-school teachers for black rural schools in Mississippi. It was through her efforts that six black schools took part in the Civilian Pilot Training Program. It paved the way for black pilots to fight in World War II.

She used her political skill to make progress outside her own agency. She got the White House to see that blacks should also work on projects that were not focused on black interests. The selection of William Hastie as the first black federal judge was partly her doing. She was always on the lookout for a door that could be opened to blacks.

She noticed that no black newspaper was allowed to cover the White House press conferences. She got that rule dropped. When her asthma became crippling, she went into Johns Hopkins Hospital for surgery. It segregated black patients and allowed no black doctors to practice. She demanded black physicians and made the hospital put them on staff for the first time.

She was always alert to the needs of black communities. One example was her own Daytona Beach. When federal funds for a black slum clearance project got held up in Washington, she got Mrs. Roosevelt to move in. But when the funds arrived, Daytona announced it would use them instead for white housing. Mrs. Bethune quickly got the funds frozen until the town agreed to put up black housing first. Seeing what weight she carried, the local bigwigs put her on the housing board. It was the first time ever that a black was permitted to have a direct say in city affairs.

She would never allow herself to be humiliated in public. When she was attending a meeting in Birmingham, Alabama, she refused to go along with segregated seating of the audience. Whenever anyone at a conference would refer to her as "Mary Bethune," she would insist for the record upon the same courtesy that the "best" white women enjoyed: she was "Mrs. Mary McLeod Bethune."

She felt bound to her people as a whole. She was speaking at a meeting of black women, when she learned that one of the Black Cabinet, worn out from tramping America to get help for black people, had died on the job. She said, "We can't give up. We have got to continue to do it. We are not here to hold a position or to be the head of this, or that, or the other; we are here to mass our power and our thinking and our souls to see what we can do to make it better for that mass that can't speak out there. That is why we are here . . . We can't give up! We must keep on. . . ."

When the United States entered World War II, the NYA closed down. Mrs. Bethune became a special assistant to the secretary of war. She was asked to help select black women for officer training in the Women's Army Corps. Segregation was still the rule, but she did everything possible to fight it in the armed services.

She was doing too many things, said her doctor. So she resigned the presidency of her beloved college. By that time—1942—the school had 14 modern buildings, a 32-acre campus and 600 students. Later it expanded to a four-year college, with over 1000 students and 100 teachers.

At the end of the war, when the United Nations met to write its charter in San Francisco, the president sent Mrs. Bethune as a consultant to the American delegation.

She remained in Washington to work as president of the National Council of Negro Women. In 1949, she resigned and retired to her cottage on the campus in Daytona Beach. Six years later, in May 1955, she died at home, in her eightieth year. She had lived long enough to see segregated education given its final blow by the Supreme Court's 1954 decision: it ruled that blacks must be admitted to public schools without discrimination. She was buried on the campus of Bethune-Cookman College.

Everyone who knew Mrs. Bethune spoke in awe of her. There was an iron fist in that velvet glove. She struck hard for whatever she believed in. She marched, she picketed, she boycotted, she signed petitions, she made speeches, she fought for laws to stop lynching and to end the poll tax and to set up fair employment practices. She did not bully or insult people she disagreed with. She made marvelous use of homely stories—as Abraham Lincoln did—to drive home a point, and she always appealed to a sense of fair play. No wonder she was called "The First Lady of the Strug-

gle." A noted journalist named her one of the ten most important women in America.

If you add it up, it's clear she helped make a revolution in what people expected of America. What did get changed in her lifetime was limited. But she proved change was possible. After her, blacks could and did push forward. The great civil rights struggle of the 1950s and '60s was powered by what Mary McLeod Bethune had set in motion.

When Mrs. Bethune died, she left a son, a grandson and six great-grandchildren. They were able to grow up in a world vastly different from the world she was born into. And in many of the ways it was better, it was better because she had done her work so well.

## ABOUT THIS BOOK

The first time I heard of Mary McLeod Bethune was in the 1930s, during the Great Depression. I was working on the Federal Theatre Project, one of the New Deal agencies providing jobs for unemployed people like myself. The newspapers talked about the great influence this remarkable black woman had on the White House and Congress. That was something new in those days, and it caught people's attention.

Mine especially, because shortly before, as a college student, I joined groups trying to do something about civil rights. We put up sidewalk stands and tried to get people to sign petitions for laws against lynching and the poll tax.

Later, when I began to write about black history, I worked with Langston Hughes. He told me of how much Mrs. Bethune had meant to him when he was young. To write this biography, I read the few books about her long out of print. Then I went to the Schomburg Center for Research in Black Culture in Harlem, New York, and read everything I could find by or about her. Just as I finished this book, the U.S. government issued a postage stamp with her picture engraved on it. And her home in Washington is now a museum that contains her papers.

I began this work with a considerable respect for her achievement. I ended it with the sure knowledge of her greatness as a figure in American history.          M.M.